Hull College
Libraries

This book must be returned on or before the
latest date stamped below

Produced for A & C Black by

Monkey Puzzle Media Ltd
Little Manor Farm, The Street
Brundish, Woodbridge, Suffolk IP13 8BL

Published in 2009 by

A & C Black Publishers Ltd
36 Soho Square, London W1D 3QY
www.acblack.com

Fourth edition 2009

ISBN: 978 07136 7695 2

This book is produced using paper that is made from
wood grown in managed, sustainable forests. It is
natural, renewable and recyclable. The logging and
manufacturing processes conform to the environmental
regulations of the country of origin.

Acknowledgements
Cover and inside design by James Winrow and
Tom Morris for Monkey Puzzle Media Ltd.
Cover photograph courtesy of PA Photos.
We would like to thank the following for permission to
reproduce photos: Bowlers' World pages 49, 51, 53,
54, 55, 56, 57; Bowls England pages 4, 19, 21, 23, 29,
30; Bowls International pages 13, 16, 27, 41, 47; Terry
Knight pages 7, 24, 25, 39, 42, 45; PA Photos page 59;
Howard Pryse pages 11, 18, 43; Bob Thomas/
Getty Images page 35.
Illustrations by Dave Saunders.

With many thanks to Terry Knight BEM, International
Umpire, and the English Bowls Umpires Association;
Howard Pryse from Bowls England; Bowls International
magazine; Bowlers' World magazine; and John Crowther
from the British Crown Green Bowling Association.

KNOW THE GAME is a registered trademark.

Printed and bound in China by C&C Offset Printing
Co., Ltd.

Note: Throughout the book players and officials are
referred to as 'he'. This should, of course, be taken
to mean 'he or she' where appropriate. Similarly, all
instructions are geared towards right-handed players –
left-handers should simply reverse these instructions.

CONTENTS

THE GREEN

The green should be at least 31m and not longer than 40m. It is divided into numbered rinks, each between 4.3m and 5.8m wide.

The green must be level and surrounded by a ditch and bank that rises at least 230mm above the green level. The surface of the bank facing the green should not be capable of damaging the jack or the bowls.

SPEED OF THE GREEN

A green is said to be 'fast' if:

- its surface is quite firm and hard
- its grass is closely mown
- it has been subjected to long periods of hot sunshine
- it has been well trodden.

A green is said to be 'slow' if:

- its grass is comparatively long
- its surface is spongy
- there has been recent heavy rainfall.

The speed of the green at indoor clubs will vary according to the type of carpet and underlay that are in use.

MARKING OUT RINKS

The four corners of the rinks are marked by pegs of wood, painted white and fixed to the face of the bank. These corner pegs should be connected with green thread drawn tightly along the surface of the green. The pegs and thread define the boundary of the rink.

▶ A good example of a flat green shown at this match of Nottinghamshire against Cumbria.

SPEED AND DISTANCE

It may sound odd but a bowl takes longer to reach its target on a 'fast' green than on a 'slow' green. On a fast green, the bowl must be delivered on a wide arc of travel (see diagram) so it has to travel a longer distance. On slow greens, a tighter arc is required. For instance, a bowl might take 10 or 11 seconds to cover a distance of 27m on a 'slow' green, whereas on a 'fast' green it might take 14 or 15 seconds to cover the same distance (see diagram below).

Weather conditions affect outdoor greens. Bowlers have to judge the conditions which can change the speed of the green even during a game.

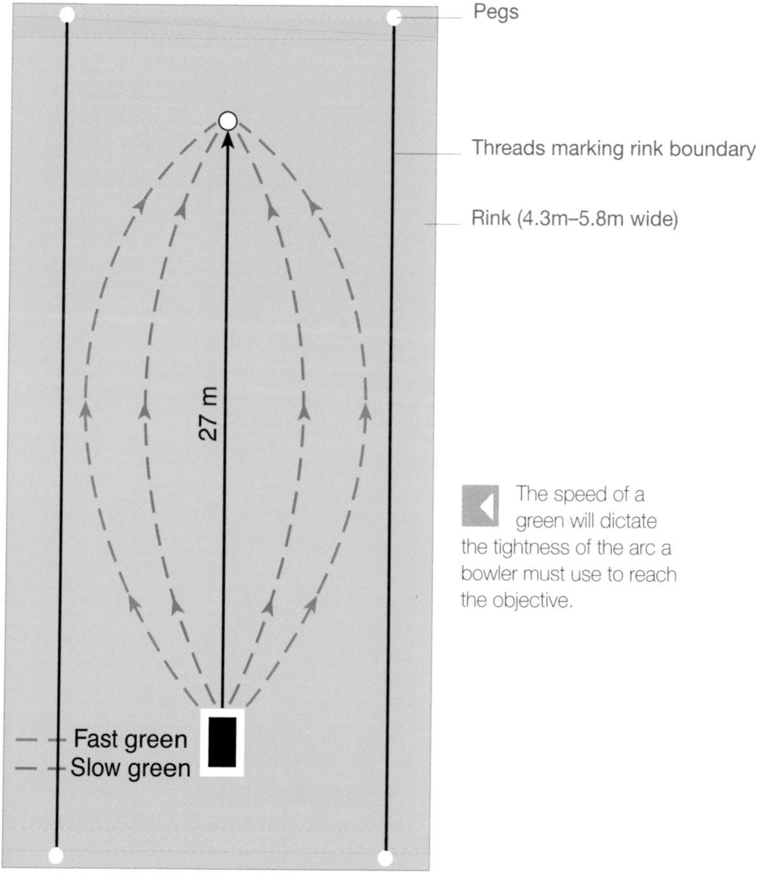

Pegs

Threads marking rink boundary

Rink (4.3m–5.8m wide)

27 m

— Fast green
— Slow green

The speed of a green will dictate the tightness of the arc a bowler must use to reach the objective.

5

EQUIPMENT

It is well known that every sport has its own individual equipment, the majority of which should be provided by the club that is joined. However, it is important that the bowler chooses the right set of bowls that suits him best. The majority of bowlers find that the set they choose will last them throughout their bowling career.

THE MAT

The mat is always placed lengthwise on the centre line of the rink. If moved during play it is replaced as close as possible to its original position.

At the start of the first end, the mat is placed with the front edge 2m from the ditch. In all subsequent ends, the mat is placed so that its front edge is at least 2m from the rear ditch and no closer than 23m from the front ditch.

Four bowls is the maximum number any one player in any one game requires.

THE JACK

The jack should be round, white, 63–64mm in diameter and between 225g and 285g in weight. The jack has no bias (see page 8). Casting a jack (see page 13) is an important skill, especially for singles players and for those playing lead (see page 24) as it can be sent the distance which most suits the casting player.

THE BOWLS

The bowls are made of wood, rubber or composition in sets of four. Each set must carry an individual distinguishing mark.

Bowls come in different weights and sizes. It is an advantage to use as heavy a bowl as possible without overloading the grip (see page 10). The choice of bowl is influenced by the grip the player uses and the size of their hand.

A new set of bowls will serve you well but can be expensive. Second-hand sets can often be bought at a reasonable price.

Lignum vitae bowls

Some bowls are made from a hard, heavy wood called lignum vitae. These must have a diameter between 116 and 134mm and a maximum weight of 1.59kg. Lignum vitae bowls are generally more responsive to bias and are less affected by heavy greens. When they lose their polish, they can also lose weight when exposed to the sun.

Composition bowls

Composition bowls are heavier, size for size, than lignum vitae bowls. They are also unaffected by temperature changes but tend to be less responsive to bias.

CHOOSING YOUR BOWLS

When buying bowls remember that:

- the bowl must not be too large for your hand
- a composition bowl is heavier than a lignum bowl
- the set should be matched – all made together from the same log. Check by looking for the set number stamped on each bowl
- seek advice from an experienced coach and/or player.

BIAS

If you examine a bowl you will see that it is not perfectly round and has a 'bias' which is built into the shape of the bowl during manufacture by careful shaping. You can see that it is slightly lower on the biased side and it is that 'built in' bias that will allow the bowl to travel in a curve.

The bias of a bowl means that it traces a curving path when rolled along level ground. The amount of curve increases as the bowl's speed decreases.

To bring a bowl to rest touching the jack, the player must aim to the left or right of it, delivering the bowl with its biased side on the right or the left. The bias side of the bowl will always be on the inside of the curve.

BIAS REGULATIONS

Every bowl has a bias, which affects the curve it follows when bowled. The amount of bias is strictly regulated and minimum levels are approved by the World Bowls Board (WBB). Each bowl must carry the stamp of the WBB/IBB and/or the British Isles Bowls Council (BIBC). Only an official tester may alter the bias.

Point of aim

The effect of the bias is barely noticeable until the bowl has covered about three-fifths of its path. From that point onwards, the bowl follows a curving path, the amount of the curve increasing all the time until the bowl comes to rest.

At three-fifths of its journey, the bowl is at its widest point from the straight line running between the mat and jack. This is known as the point of aim. Fixing the point of aim will vary with each bowl sent down the green. It depends upon:

• the length of the jack, i.e. distance from mat to jack

• the bias on the bowl

• the wind

• the heaviness of the green – on a wet, heavy green less land will be used than on a dry green

• the trueness of the green – one side of the green might 'draw' (see page 32) better than the other side.

The bias side of the bowl is indicated by the smaller of the two discs stamped into the bowl. The bias should always be on the inside for forehand and backhand shots.

Always test the green, sending a few bowls down from each end and from both directions, before beginning play. In competitive games trial ends before the game starts are allowed.

LAND

The area enclosed between the curved path of the bowl and the line from the mat to the jack is known as 'land' (also called 'line', 'width', 'green' or 'grass').

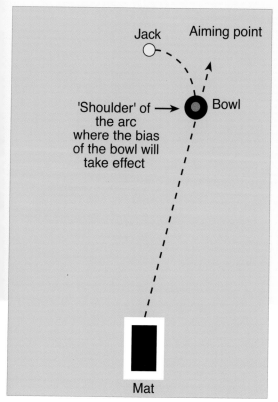

Jack   Aiming point

Bowl

'Shoulder' of the arc where the bias of the bowl will take effect

Mat

This diagram shows the point of aim in relation to the jack.

GRIP AND DELIVERY

It is important to choose the grip that suits you. In bowls there are two basic grips – the claw and the cradle. The claw grip is the one most widely used and is suitable for all conditions, whereas the cradle grip is used more on heavier greens. It must be remembered that if the bowl is not held properly it will not leave the hand properly and smoothly and you will get into bad habits.

CLAW GRIP

In the claw grip, much of the palm is not in contact with the bowl which is held mainly by the thumb and fingers. The thumb is placed on or near the top of the bowl. The fingers are spread evenly on the underside, reasonably close together. The little finger is occasionally brought up the bowl on the opposite side to the thumb.

Whichever grip is used, make sure the bowl can be held upright so that it is not leaning to the left or right.

Avoid strain on the wrist and the thumb's base by not overgripping or squeezing the bowl.

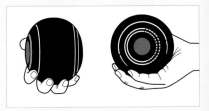

CRADLE GRIP

The cradle grip is, as its name implies, where the bowl is cradled in the palm of the hand with the fingers closer together and both the thumb and the little finger resting on the side of the bowl – this grip is more suitable for use with a larger bowl or on a slower green.

Catherine Popple showing her grip and stance on the mat.

The forehand (curves inwards from the right-hand side) and backhand (curves inwards from left-hand side) shots for a right-handed bowler.

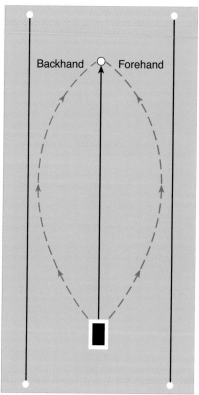

Backhand   Forehand

DELIVERY

Aim for good balance during the stance. This may be helped by keeping the feet apart. Do not overgrip the bowl. During the backswing, keep the bowling arm as close to the hips as possible to allow an even pendulum movement. Do not let the bowl travel away from or behind the body. The forward swing of the bowling arm, forward step and forward movement of the body, should all be smooth and controlled. Make sure the knees are bent enough to allow the body to be close to the playing surface. This ensures the bowl is released smoothly without wobble or bounce. Complete the delivery action with a flowing follow through.

Stance and foot faults

A player must take a stance on the mat and at the moment of delivery, must have one foot in contact with or over the mat. Failure to do so means the player has foot-faulted and that bowl is stopped and removed to the bank.

THE GAME

Like many games the object of bowls is really quite simple and can be played by almost everyone. However, to play well and to be consistent, it is necessary to be determined, to concentrate at all times and to practise. To be successful the bowl must be delivered with the correct weight, along the correct line, and to ensure that one or more bowls get closer to the jack than those of the opposition.

TYPES OF GAME

A single game is restricted to one rink and features between one and four players a side.

There are, in addition, three other arrangements of play:

- a side game – played over several rinks by two opposing sides, each side having the same number of players

- a series of single or team games arranged either as knockout or league competitions and accommodating single-handed, pairs, triples or fours

- a tournament of games in which the competing sides or teams play each other in turn.

No. of players per side	Name
One	single-handed or singles
Two	pairs
Three	triples
Four	fours

STARTING THE GAME

The captains in a side game or skips in a team game toss to decide which side plays first. In all singles games, the winner chooses who plays first. In all ends after the first, the winner of the previous scoring end should choose whether to:

a) place the mat and deliver the jack and first bowl, or

b) tell the opposing player to place the mat and deliver the jack and first bowl. The opposing player cannot refuse.

Players and spectators enjoying a game.

Casting the jack

The player to play first casts the jack. If the jack comes to rest less than 2m from the front ditch, it is moved to 2m from that ditch and centred. Improper delivery of the jack occurs when:

- the jack travels into the ditch
- travels outside the rink boundary
- travels less than 21m in a straight line from the front of the mat.

If this occurs, the opposing player may remove the mat in line of play (see page 6), deliver the jack but does not play first.

If the jack is improperly delivered twice by each player in one end, it is centred 2m from the opposite ditch.

THE SINGLES GAME

A singles game should be played between two opposing players. Each player has four bowls which they bowl one at a time, alternating with their opponent. Once all bowls have been delivered, all bowls nearer to the jack than an opponent's nearest bowl count one shot each. The maximum score for an end is four.

Once the end is completed and the shots have been agreed, a fresh end begins by playing back along the rink. The first player to reach 21 shots wins the game.

THE PAIRS GAME

A pairs game should be played by two opposing teams, each with two players. Each player has four bowls and plays them singly and in turn (see diagram). All bowls of one pair nearer to the jack than any bowl of the two opponents count one shot each. The maximum score for an end is eight shots. The game finishes when the agreed number of ends have been played. The pair with the highest score are the winners.

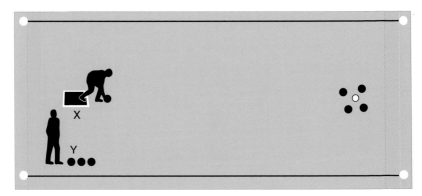

Player **X** in this singles game delivers the jack and then their first bowl. Player **Y**, then delivers their first bowl, after which player **X** follows and so on until both players have delivered their four bowls.

THE TRIPLES GAME

A triples game should be played by two opposing teams, each with three players. Each player usually has three bowls. The first players of each team deliver their bowls alternately, followed by the second players in each team and, finally, the third. All bowls of one team nearer to the jack than any of the three opponents count one shot each with a maximum score per end of nine. The game usually finishes when the agreed number of ends have been played. The highest scoring team win.

THE FOURS GAME

Each side consists of four players, each player having two bowls and playing them singly and in turn. All bowls of one team nearer to the jack than any bowl of the four opponents count one shot each. The game concludes in the same way as the triples game, the team with the highest score being the winners.

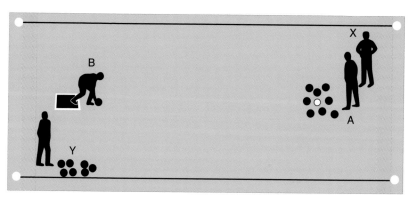

In this pairs game, **A** and **B** are playing **X** and **Y**. **A** and **X** alternate until they have each delivered four bowls; then **B** and **Y** alternate until they have sent down four bowls each.

MOVEMENT OF BOWLS

When a bowl has been properly delivered by a player and comes to rest, it is said to be either live or dead. If it touches the jack during its course it becomes a toucher. A bowl which does not touch the jack is a non-toucher.

LIVE BOWL

A bowl which travels 14m or more from the front of the mat and comes to rest within the boundaries of the rink is called a live bowl. A live bowl is in play.

DEAD BOWL

A dead bowl is one which:

- travels less than 14m from the front of the mat

- finishes in the ditch not having touched the jack

- comes to rest so that the whole of the bowl is outside the boundaries of the rink

- or has been driven beyond the side boundaries of the rink by another bowl.

A toucher (see page 18–19) becomes a dead bowl if it:

- comes to rest so that the whole of the bowl is outside the boundaries of the rink or

- has been driven beyond the side boundaries of the rink by another bowl.

IN AND OUT OF THE RINK

A bowl can travel beyond the side boundary of the rink and return into the rink if part or all of the bowl comes to rest inside the rink.

A bowl must be removed from the rink and placed on the bank immediately it is accounted dead. Should a player carry a bowl to the jack end of the rink, that bowl does not become a dead one.

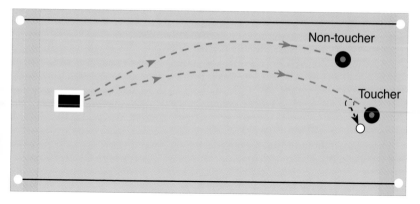

A live bowl must travel at least 14m from the front of the mat.

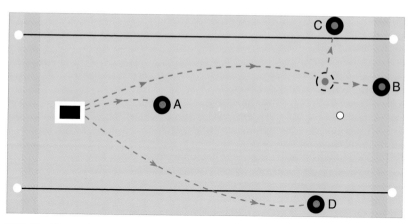

Dead bowls. Bowl **A** has not travelled 14m. Bowl **B** has come to rest outside of the rink. Bowl **C** has been driven beyond the rink's side boundaries. Bowl **D** has come to rest outside the boundary of the rink.

A toucher is marked using chalk moments after it has come to rest.

A boundary thread must not be lifted while the bowl is in motion.

17

TOUCHERS

A bowl which, in its original course on the green, makes contact with the jack is called a toucher (see page 17). It remains a 'live' bowl even if it passes into the ditch, provided it comes to rest in that part of the ditch within the rink's boundaries.

If the jack is driven into the ditch by a toucher and comes to rest there, no subsequent bowl in the end being played can become a toucher.

If toucher marks are left on by mistake for a new end, they should be removed when the bowl has been delivered and come to rest.

MARKING A TOUCHER

A toucher shall be clearly marked or indicated with a chalk mark by a member of the player's side. If a toucher is not marked before the next bowl is delivered, it becomes a non-toucher. A toucher in the ditch may be marked by a white or a coloured peg placed upright on the top of the bank. The peg is about 50mm broad and not more than 100mm in height.

International umpire, Terry Knight, makes some measurements at a tense moment.

TOUCHER AND JACK IN THE DITCH

Certain rules apply to a toucher when the jack is in the ditch. If the jack is in the ditch and is later displaced by another, non-toucher, bowl, it is restored to its original position in the ditch.

The jack in the ditch is not restored if it is displaced by:

- a toucher on the green later driven by another bowl into the ditch where it hits the jack

- a toucher in the ditch driven by another toucher into displacing the jack.

REBOUNDING BOWLS

Touchers which rebound from the bank to the rink remain live bowls and continue in play. Non-touchers which rebound from the bank, from the jack or touchers lying in the ditch are dead bowls.

Always remove toucher marks before playing the next end.

 A careful check of the bowl's position is vital.

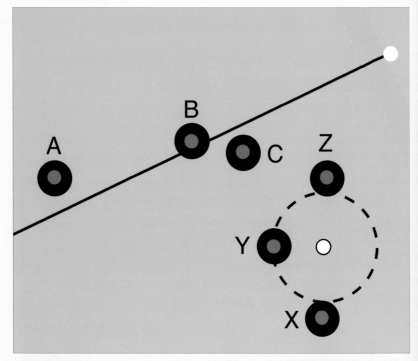

LINE BOWLS

A bowl has to be entirely clear of a line or circle to be considered outside of it. This is decided by looking down on the bowl directly from above or by using a string, mirror or another approved, optical device.

Bowl **A** is entirely beyond the side boundary and is dead. Bowl **C** is entirely inside and is live. Bowl **B** lies partly over the side boundary thread and is also live. The circle around the jack represents the inner edge of the bowl **Z**. Bowl **X** is outside the circle and is furthest from the jack whilst bowl **Y** lies partly over the circle and is nearest.

DISPLACED BOWLS

If a bowl is displaced from its position by a non-toucher rebounding from the bank it should be restored as near as possible to its original position. This task is performed by an opposition player.

If a player taking part in the game interferes with a moving bowl or displaces a live bowl at rest, the captain of the opposing side can do one of four things:

- restore the bowl as near as possible to its former position

- let it remain where it rests

- declare the bowl dead

- declare the end dead.

If a bowl is moved when being marked or measured, an opponent must restore it to its former position. If a marker or umpire causes the displacement, then they should replace the bowl.

BY CAPTAINS' AGREEMENT

A moving bowl may be interfered with or a live bowl at rest displaced from its former position by the following agents:

- an object lying on the green

- a bowl played from another rink

- a person not playing on the rink.

In these situations, the bowl should be placed in a position acceptable to the two captains. If they cannot reach agreement, the end becomes dead and is replayed in the same direction.

Take great care not to disturb live bowls until the end has been completed and shots awarded.

Two teams contemplate the result following the delivery of a bowl.

JACK MOVEMENT

In any game, the start of play is the delivery of the jack by the first player to play in the first end. When the team managers of a side game have tossed a coin and made the decision who should play first, it will apply to all of the rinks in that side. If a jack is delivered from an illegally placed mat, it should be returned and re-delivered by the opposing player, who can reset the mat. No one can challenge the position of the mat once the first bowl has been delivered.

Live jack in a ditch

A jack driven into the rink's part of the ditch remains live and its position is marked with a white peg (50mm wide and no taller than 100mm) placed in the bank.

Boundary jack

A jack driven to the side boundary, but not wholly beyond it, remains live. Players can play to the jack from either side, even if their bowl passes outside of the rink. However, it must come to rest partly or wholly inside the side boundary.

Dead jack

The jack becomes dead if it is driven by the bowl in play:

- over the bank

- over the side boundary

- into an opening in the bank or

- so that it rebounds to a distance less than 20m from the centre of the front edge of the mat.

When the jack is dead, the end is declared dead even if all bowls have been played. It must be replayed, usually in the same direction unless both skips or opponents agree to play in the opposite direction. If the end is declared dead the player that cast the original jack in that end re-starts it.

Damaged jack

If the jack is damaged during play, the end is declared dead and is played again in the same direction using a new jack.

Rebounding jack

If the jack is driven against the bank and rebounds on to the rink it remains in play. If the jack is lying in the ditch and is propelled by a toucher back onto the rink, it also remains in play.

Jacks surrounded by bowls in play in three separate games.

Displaced jack

The jack is restored to its original position by an opponent if:

- it is displaced from its position by a non-toucher rebounding from the bank

- it was in the ditch and has been displaced by a non-toucher.

Should a moving jack on the green be diverted or a jack at rest is disturbed by an opponent, then captains of the opposing side have three choices. They may:

- have the jack restored to its former position

- allow it to remain where it rests or

- declare the end dead.

A jack, moving or at rest, which suffers displacement by a bowl from another rink, an object lying on the green or a person not playing on the rink must be replaced. Its position should be agreed by the two captains. If no agreement is reached, the end is dead.

> **A jack that is driven partly over a boundary thread, but not wholly beyond it, is live.**

WRONG TEAM DELIVERS THE JACK

If the wrong team delivers the jack and only one bowl has been delivered, then the end is restarted by the correct team.

If each team has delivered one bowl, then the end continues in the 'incorrect' order of play.

FOURS PLAY

Singles, pairs and triple games are all popular but the basis of the game of bowls is fours play. Fours has the advantage of accommodating the maximum number of players – eight – per rink. Each player in fours play is limited to two bowls, and with only a pair of bowls to deliver in each end, no player can afford to be careless with either shot.

The four players in each team are known as lead, second, third and skip. They play in that order, alternating their shots with their opposite numbers in the other teams. Each position demands certain skills and duties of the player.

The lead

The lead places the mat, delivers the jack and ensures the jack is centred before delivering the first bowl. If the lead's side has won the preceding end, the jack can be delivered to the winning four's preferred length – a big advantage.

The lead needs to be skilled at playing to any length of jack and must aim to get both bowls nearer the jack than the opponent's. The choice of hands – backhand or forehand – rests with the lead, who should decide which hand most suits the four.

> Don't change the playing order during a game as this can lead to forfeiting the match to your opponents.

A team must work together efficiently if they are to be successful.

The second

The second holds possession of the scorecard throughout the game. As scorer, seconds must:

- record the players' names

- record all shots for and against their side

- compare their record of the game with the opposing second after each end and hand the scorecard to their skip at the game's completion.

As a player, the second specialises in positioning. If the lead has placed a bowl nearest the jack, the second should play the bowl into a protecting position. If the lead has lost the shot, seconds attempt to place their bowls closest to the jack. Versatility is required of the second, who must be able to play almost any shot in the game.

In this photograph taken at the England v Wales International (2008), the Welsh skip (Wendy Price) can be seen with her lead and second encouraging their third player. All players are standing behind the head. Note the stickers on the bowls – red for Wales and blue for England.

The third

The third player may be given the duty of measuring all disputed shots. The third needs to be an experienced player, who must be ready for forceful play but who can, when necessary, play any shot in the game.

The skip

Skips have sole charge of their rink, and their instructions must be obeyed by their players. The skip decides, with the opposing skip, all disputed points, and their agreed decision is final. If the two skips disagree, the disputed point is referred to an umpire whose decision is final.

Skips play last. While their players are delivering their bowls, skips issue directions to them by hand movements. The skip decides the four's tactics and strategy.

POSITION OF PLAYERS DURING PLAY

Possession of the rink belongs to each side in turn, belonging, at any moment, to the side whose bowl is being played. As soon as each bowl comes to rest, possession of the rink is transferred to the other side. There is one exception to this rule – when a bowl becomes a toucher. In this situation, possession is not transferred until the toucher has been marked.

The position of players during play is important. The end/part of the green where the jack is located,

An excellent example of players behind the head and spectators not interfering with play. Taken at the Middleton Cup match at Worthing with Gloucestershire v Huntingdonshire.

which can be the ditch, is known as the head. Players standing at the head of the green, unless directing play, must stand behind the jack and away from the head.

The skip or third man directing play may stand in front of the jack, but must retire behind it as soon as the bowl is delivered.

All players at the mat end of the green, other than the one actually delivering a bowl, must stand behind the mat.

Players not in possession of the rink must not interfere with their opponents, distract their attention, or in any way annoy them.

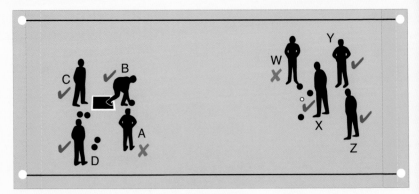

CORRECT AND INCORRECT POSITIONS

In the illustration, Player A, having played the bowl, is standing in front of the mat, though to one side. This is distracting, though not obstructing, player B. The Laws of the Sport of Bowls say that A should stand back, behind the mat, like C and D.

At the head of the green, players X and Y are standing in proper positions. Although standing to one side of the jack, player W is still in front of the jack. W should stand behind the jack, behind X, who is skip to B.

Correct and incorrect position of players in fours play.

A bowl played by mistake shall be replaced with the player's own bowl by the opponent.

CHANGING BOWLS

Players are not allowed to change their bowls during the course of the game, or in a resumed game unless a bowl has been damaged during play and in the opinion of the umpire is unfit to play.

Bowls must not be used if they become damaged during a game.

PLAYING OUT OF TURN

1. If a player plays out of turn, the opposing skip can stop the bowl and return it to the player to play in the proper order.

2. If the bowl has come to rest and has not disturbed the head, the opposing skip should choose whether to:

- leave the disturbed head as it is and have their team play two bowls one after the other to get back to the proper order of play

- return the bowl and get back to the proper order of play.

3. If the bowl has disturbed the head, the opposing skip should choose whether to:

- leave the disturbed head as it is and have their team play two bowls one after the other to get back to the proper order of play

- replace the head in its former position, return the bowl and get back to the proper order of play

- declare the end dead.

INTERRUPTIONS

The umpire may stop a game, or the teams may mutually agree to cease play, on account of the weather, or because of darkness. When the game is resumed the score will be as it was when the interruption occurred. An end that was not completed before the interruption should not be counted. When the game is resumed, if one of the four original players is not available, a substitute player is allowed.

RESULT OF THE END

To allow all the bowls to come finally to rest, up to half a minute after the last bowl has stopped running may be claimed by either side before counting the shots to allow the last bowl played, if leaning to fall over and so become the winning shot bowl. No bowl that is likely to fall should be wedged during that period.

The jack or bowls may not be moved until the skips have agreed the number of shots except where one bowl must be moved to allow the measuring of another.

Scoring Bowls

Scoring bowls are ones nearer to the jack than any of the opponents' bowls. In a game of winning ends the side with the bowl nearest the jack in each end becomes the winner of that end. Otherwise all bowls nearer the jack than any of the opponents' bowls count one shot each.

MEASURING BOWLS

Great care must be taken when measuring a bowl to ensure that the positions of other bowls are not disturbed. If the bowl to be measured is resting on another bowl, players must use the best means to secure it in its position before removing the other bowl. Similar action should be taken where more than two bowls are involved or where measurement is likely to cause a single bowl to fall over or change its position.

Tallying the score!

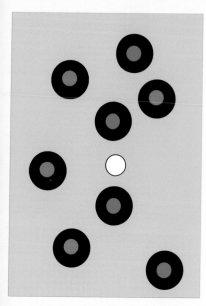

The blue team has two bowls nearer the jack than the red team. The blue team scores 2 shots. If played as 'winning ends', the blue team scores 1 shot.

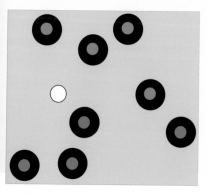

The blue team has one bowl nearer the jack than the red team. The blue team scores 1 shot. If played as 'winning ends', the blue team scores 1 shot.

If the nearest bowl of each team is touching the jack, or are agreed to be the same distance from the jack, the end is a draw and no score is recorded.

GAME DECISIONS

In a game of winning ends, the victory decision goes to the side or team with the most winning ends. For other games, the victory decision goes to the side or team with the highest total of shots. The above decisions apply to:

- a single game
- a team or side game played on one occasion
- any stage of an eliminating competition.

In tournament games, or games in series, victory goes to the side or team with the most winning ends or highest net score of shots, according to the rules of the tournament or series of games.

If, in an eliminating competition, the score is equal when the agreed number of ends has been played, an extra end or ends are played until there is a winner.

SHOTS

During your early days in learning to play the game, it is most important to practise the draw shot, which really is the 'bread and butter' of the game. To see your bowl end up next to the jack time and time again, is a most rewarding experience and is the means by which you will win a game more often than not. As you gain in experience and become more confident with your game, you can start to use the various other shots, all of which must be carefully selected when you assess your chances.

DRAW SHOT

Drawing a bowl is delivering it along the correct line and with enough pace or weight to reach the objective. It is the most basic but most important shot in a bowler's repertoire. Draw shots are not just bowled to the jack but can be played to an opponent's bowl or to a particular spot on the rink. The following shots, plus the plant and blocking shot on page 37, are variations on the draw shot.

Trail shot

A trailing shot carries the jack from one position on the rink to another. In the diagram, the bowler has used enough pace for the bowl to carry the jack from point **Y** to point **X**.

Rest shot

Here the bowler has played the shot so that the bowl comes to rest against the opponent's bowl (**A**). This can sometimes help to increase the number of scoring bowls or may provide some form of 'insurance' against opponents moving the jack to their own bowl.

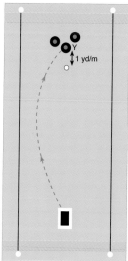

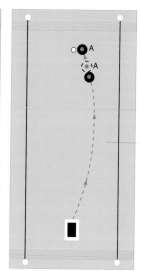

Wrest shot

The object of a wrest shot is to displace an opponent's bowl, ensuring that your bowl takes its place.

Yard on shot

In a yard on shot, the bowler delivers the bowl so that it comes to rest at point **Y**, a yard (1m) behind the jack.

Promotion shot

Here the bowler wishes to push the bowl (**A**) closer to the jack. Assessing the correct weight of the delivery is vital. If the target bowl to be displaced is on its side, then a little more weight is required.

Ditch weight shot

Here the jack is in the ditch and live. The bowler delivers the bowl with enough pace to make it come to rest at the lip of the ditch. The bowl should not fall into the ditch. If it does so, it becomes dead.

CONTROLLED WEIGHT SHOTS

Generally speaking, playing with controlled weight means that even if the shot misses its target or targets, the bowl remains on the rink and in play. The split and opening up shots are two which require controlled force.

Opening up shot

This is a shot played with sufficient pace to move bowls that have come to rest between the bowler and the jack (see above). This shot is occasionally necessary to create more options for the next shot.

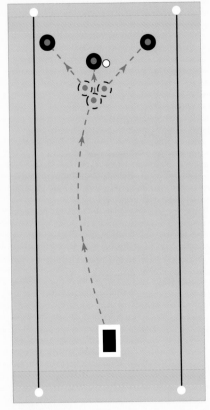

Split shot

In the diagram above the bowler dislodges the opponent's bowls (blue) by playing with sufficient force. The bowler's bowl (red) travels on towards the jack and becomes the shot bowl.

Remember to adjust your line when playing controlled or firing pace shots. The greater the speed of the bowl, the narrower or tighter the line.

Drive or firing shot

This is a bowl delivered at optimum pace to achieve one of several objectives:

- to drive the jack out of the confines of the rink and 'kill' the end

- to play into a group of your opponent's bowls to drive them out of the head and thereby reduce the opponent's score

- to scatter the bowls in a head that is building against you

- to take out an opponent's bowl that is preventing you scoring a number of shots.

David Bryant, the world's most successful bowler, was well-known for using the drive shot.

TACTICS

No two ends in bowls are exactly the same. To be able to exploit all the options, players need to be well prepared and have a wide variety of shots at their disposal. Strategy can change from one end to another, and more versatile players have the greater chance of shifting play to their advantage. One end can change the course or pattern of any game, so no matter what an opponent is doing bowlers must always attempt to be disciplined and controlled.

FIRST BOWL

In very basic terms, players need to get more of their bowls in a scoring position than their opponent. Players about to play the first bowl must be clear as to where they wish the bowl to come to rest. Correct line and length are crucial. A bowl just behind or just in front of the jack represents a good start.

An opponent could react in several different ways by:

- attempting to draw even closer to the jack

- moving the first bowl

- trailing the jack away from the first bowl.

Shot selection and tactics are decided by where the first bowl comes to rest. So it can continue with each bowler attempting to wrest the advantage away from their opponent. Such play calls for effective decision making.

MAXIMISE AND MINIMISE

It is vital that players strive to maximise shots for and to minimise shots against. To draw an end, for example, when there was previously a high count against is important and can result in a boost in confidence.

PRE-VISUALISATION

Some bowlers employ a pre-visualisation technique before delivering a bowl. They 'see' their bowl travelling along the green and they have a definite and clear picture of it coming to rest at a precise spot. This technique is particularly important when a bowl has to travel around a bowl, or pass through a gap between bowls.

READING AN OPPONENT

From the first moment bowlers try
to read opponents, building up a
picture of their playing abilities
and style:

- what are their strengths
  and weaknesses

- how do they respond to good
  and bad luck

- are they stronger on one hand
  than the other

- do they prefer to play a
  particular hand or length?

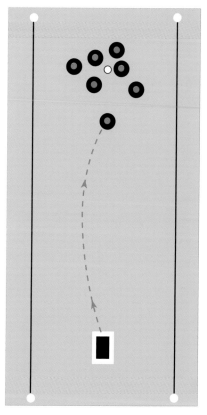

A blocking shot is a drawing shot
which comes to rest some way
short of the head. It is used to protect
an advantage or to prevent an opponent
breaking up the head.

A plant shot occurs
where a bowler strikes
their own bowl (**A**) with
enough pace to dislodge
an opponent's bowl (**B**).

COMMON FAULTS

Nothing is more frustrating than seeing your bowl end up very short of the jack, going off-line or ending in the ditch, despite your best efforts. There are many reasons why things go wrong, the most common of which is lack of concentration and self-discipline. Training sessions with a qualified bowls instructor should help you to solve the majority of your errors, but you must be prepared to acknowledge your mistakes and do your best to overcome them if your game is to improve.

GRIP

It is vital that the grip is a comfortable one that offers control.

Problem: bowl wobbles on release

Bowl leaning to right or left in hand? Make sure it is upright.

Little finger position too high on side of bowl. If so, lower it.

> Limit any unnecessary physical movement once the stance is adopted. Keep the whole motion simple and straightforward.

STANCE

A solid stance provides a well balanced and relaxed platform for the smooth delivery of the bowl. Height, weight, general build and the suppleness of knee, hip, wrist and shoulder joints all play a part in the stance chosen.

Problem: loss of balance

Ensure feet are not too close together. This will narrow your base and can lead to loss of stability.

Problem: loss of line when bowling

Is stance and body aligned on the mat with the path the bowl is to take? If not, align carefully. For a right-handed player the right foot should point along the selected line, then the left foot can be brought alongside it.

BACKSWING

The backswing is a simple pendulum movement backwards with the bowling arm travelling close to the hip on its journey.

Avoid holding the bowl away from your body before the backswing as this can result in the bowling arm travelling a long distance away from the body.

Also avoid holding the ball in front of your body before starting your backswing. This can lead to the bowl being hidden behind the body at the end of the backswing and can lead to an outward curve in the forward swing and a less accurate delivery. It is better for the elbow of the bowling arm to rest close to the hip, with the bowl pointing along the right line.

 This Welsh player is using the backswing.

Problem: wrong length

Is your backswing short and does not pass by your hip? This can result in the bowl being pushed rather than rolled away, often leading to unsatisfactory length. It is easier to feel a better weight control with a smooth pendulum forward movement than with a pushing action. Make sure your backswing is smooth and long.

Increased weight and the backswing

Many players lengthen their backswing when playing an increased weight shot. This can sometimes lead to an undesirable jerky delivery rather than a smooth action. The backswing should always be controlled, and if extra pace or weight is needed then the bowler should concentrate on bringing the bowling arm through at a faster rate. Make sure, though, that the faster forward action does not lead to a forward lunge of the body and a loss of balance.

FORWARD STEP

The timing and style of forward step varies. Some bowlers take it at the same time as the backswing. Others, as they are completing the forward swing. Some players split the forward stride into two movements by placing the leading foot ahead of the back foot even before they begin the backswing. On completion of the forward swing, only a small forward movement is then needed by the leading foot.

Problem: overlong forward stride

This can add a lot of body weight to the delivery action which if not controlled well can result in a poor shot. An excessively long forward stride can also cause a player to lose some balance. Adjust your forward stride to that of a regular stride at walking pace. Also consider bending your knees. This lowers the body and makes it more difficult to take a long forward stride.

Bending the knees helps to lower the body closer to the green to ensure a smooth release of the bowl.

FORWARD SWING

The required pace determines how fast the arm comes through on the forward swing, but it should always be under control. The forward swing should also always be smooth, unhurried and disciplined. Any jerkiness in movement will result in a poorly delivered bowl. During the swing, the shoulder, elbow, wrist and hand of the bowling arm must face the chosen line. The arm should therefore be kept close to the body.

Problem: bowl lobbed out of the hand rather than rolled

Are you accelerating the speed of your bowling arm in the last part of its swing? If so, try to keep the forward swing smooth and equal paced throughout.

THE WRONG FOOT

Because of problems with knee or hip joints, some players elect to play off the 'wrong' foot, i.e. a right-handed player steps forwards with the right foot. This does not contravene any law.

PLACING FORWARD FOOT

The placing of the forward foot is vital for a smooth delivery and must point down the line taken towards the 'aiming point' (see page 9) – this is known as the line of delivery.

Problem: forward foot placed at an angle across the body

On both the forehand and backhand side this may result in the bowling arm following an incorrect line. Make sure your front foot points correctly and not across your body.

THE OTHER HAND

When delivering the bowl, make sure that the other hand does not wave about in an aimless manner. It is important to remember that your body should be as stable as possible – 'as steady as a rock'.

To ensure that you are stable grasp the thigh of the front leg firmly as this will then prevent any swaying or loss of balance as the bowl is delivered.

Problem: uneven delivery

When bowling the body should be well-balanced and the legs must be free from tension – try to keep the knees relaxed and keep your eyes firmly to a point along the line of delivery.

International player Jamie Chestney at English Men's Indoor Pairs competition at Nottingham 2008. He is using the 'cradle' grip.

RELEASE

The body must be perfectly balanced on release of the bowl.

The correct timing of the release is critical. Too soon or too late and the bowl can be bumped on delivery losing some of its required pace. The exact point of release will vary from player to player, but it should not be behind the leading foot or, indeed, too far ahead of it.

FOLLOW THROUGH

The follow through is the natural completion of the forward swing. To practise this, place a coin in the palm of your bowling hand and swing the arm forwards to lob the coin out of your hand. The palm remains uppermost with the arm pointing down the line taken by the coin's path.

Some bowlers complete the follow through by bringing their arm across their body. This can result in a hooking action if the movement is begun a fraction too early. Deliver the bowl correctly before the swing across begins.

Practise the delivery action without a bowl. The point where your fingers brush the floor is likely to be a good/natural point of release for you.

HEAD POSITION

Head position is vital. Any unnecessary movement of the head affects the shoulders, arms and your overall balance. Keep your head still yet not rigid, but as comfortable as possible. All players have an optimum distance they can look along the green with the maximum degree of comfort. Find that point. At the point of release, do not:

- drop your head and look downwards

- bob your head up swiftly.

To correct these problems, try to watch the bowl travel for at least 7–9m before bringing up your head.

NON-BOWLING ARM

The whole of the body is involved in the delivery action. The non-bowling arm should not wave about during delivery.

Smooth delivery with head up and eyes focused on aiming point. Non-bowling hand grasping thigh and knees bent.

If the bowling arm is free during delivery, it should be placed in almost the same spot each time. Alternatively it can be placed:

- on the thigh of the leading leg
- on the knee of the leading leg.

REAR LEG AND FOOT

The rear leg and foot are crucial to good balance. Many prefer to keep the foot anchored on the mat. Others raise it at the moment of release.

Some players stand at the back end of the mat and have to take a long forward step to reach the playing surface. There is nothing wrong with this unless it results in loss of balance.

Young bowlers who are sufficiently supple will keep the rear foot on the mat but allow the knee to tuck in behind the front leg. This can provide a narrow base for balance but their suppleness allows them to do this without any apparent strain or discomfort.

> **Do not get into the common habit of flicking your wrist or fingers on delivery.**

> **Try not to end your delivery action balancing on the toes of your rear foot. This could cause your body to wobble.**

Natalie Melmore (Devon) in action at the International Test England v Wales. Note her non-bowling arm resting on the thigh of her leading leg.

THE MARKER AND UMPIRE

In a singles game a good marker can help to make the game whereas a bad marker can completely ruin a game. The score should be kept by the marker who will also need chalk spray and/or chalk, a box measure, wedges and pen or pencil. A scorecard holder can be carried and can double-up as a kneeling pad if the grass is damp. Mobile phones should not be carried but locked away.

1. In the absence of an umpire, the marker should make sure that:

- the game is played in line with the Laws of the Sport of Bowls;

all bowls have a clearly visible, valid World Bowls stamp imprinted on them; the rink of play is the correct width; and the pegs or discs on the side banks in the direction of play are the correct distances.

2. The marker should:

- centre the jack and check that the jack is at least 23m from the mat line

- place a full-length jack 2m from the ditch, stand to one side of the rink, behind the jack and away from the head

- answer any specific question about the state of the head which is asked by the player in possession of the rink

- when asked, tell or show the player in possession of the rink the position of the jack and which bowl considers to be shot

- mark all touchers with chalk and remove the chalk marks from non-touchers as soon as they come to rest

- if both players agree, remove dead bowls from the rink of play

- mark the position of a jack and any touchers in the ditch

- not move, or cause to be moved, either the jack or any bowls until the players have agreed the number of shots scored

- measure any disputed shot or shots. If the players are not satisfied with the marker's decision, the marker should ask the umpire to do the measuring. If an umpire has not been appointed, the marker should choose a competent neutral person to act as the umpire. The umpire's decision is final.

Marker Peter Stewart informing a Welsh player that he is 4 shots down as Sam Tolchard (England) comes up to inspect the head.

REMOVING BOWLS

With the agreement of both opponents, the marker can remove all dead bowls from the green and ditch. He or she shall not move either the jack or bowls until each player has agreed to the number of shots.

3. When each end has been completed, the marker should:

- record the score on the scorecard

- tell the players the running totals of the scores

- remove from the rink the mat used during the previous end.

4. When the game has been completed, the marker should make sure that the scorecard contains the names and signatures of the players and the time at which the game was completed.

FURTHER RULES

No matter what sport is played it is virtually impossible to have laws that can cope with every situation, and unusual situations not covered within the laws can often arise. The Laws of the Sport of Bowls were drawn up in the spirit of true sportsmanship and if a situation arises not covered within those laws then the spirit of fair play and common sense must prevail in order to decide the most appropriate course of action. Some of the more common situations are now covered.

ABSENTEE PLAYERS

In a competitive single fours game where a club is represented by only one four, all the members of the four must be genuine members of the club. There is a maximum waiting period of 30 minutes, after which the team forfeit the match to their opponents.

In a side game where only one player is absent after a period of 30 minutes, the game proceeds but with the following conditions imposed on the defaulting team:

- the lead and second players each play three bowls

- one quarter of the score made by this team is deducted at the end of the game

- if two or more players are absent from a four or team, play takes place only on the full fours. In a single four game, the defaulting team forfeits the game.

PLAY INTERRUPTIONS

If one of the original players in any four is not available when play is resumed after an interruption, one substitute is permitted, but they must not be transferred from another four.

A substitute may also take the place of a player who has to leave the green owing to illness. The substitute must be a member of the club to which the four belongs, and must join the four as lead, second or third player – never as skip. Should a player in a single game become ill, the game is resumed, if possible, at a later time or date.

> You must not delay play by leaving the rink except with the consent of your opponent, and then not for more than ten minutes.

Game in progress showing spectators outside the rink.

If any of the following conditions are not observed, the opposing side can claim the game or match.

OUTSIDE INFLUENCES

Spectators

Spectators must remain outside the rink and clear of the verges at all times.

Objects on the green

Except for the markings of a live jack in the ditch, no other object intended to assist a player may be placed on the green or rink, or on a bowl or jack.

Unforeseen incidents

If the jack or bowls are disturbed by wind or a storm, and the two skips are unable to agree the replacement positions, the end is played again in the same direction.

Betting and gambling

Betting or gambling in connection with any game is not permitted within the grounds of any club that is a member of a national association.

THE GREEN

The green is usually square or rectangular. There is no minimum or maximum size, but the green must be large enough to allow the minimum mark of 19m to be set and the footer to be placed at least one metre from the edge of the green. Many greens have a raised crown which may be in the centre – some greens have more than one crown and some have no crown at all. The entrance to the green, which must be near the centre of one of the sides, should be clearly marked.

BOWLS, JACK AND FOOTER

Each player uses two bowls and a bowl must weigh at least 900g. Most bowls are 2 full bias. Many players have several sets of bowls. The game is played with standard jacks of 2 full bias as approved by the British Crown Green Bowling Association. Jacks manufactured before 1 January 1994 must weigh a minimum of 567g and a maximum of 680g. Jacks manufactured between 1 January 1994 and 1 March 2004 must weigh between 653g and 680g. Those made after 1 March 2004 must be black or yellow in colour and weigh 666g, plus or minus 10g. The footer must have a diameter of between 128mm and 154mm and the player's foot must be placed on it when delivering the jack or bowl.

EFFECTS OF BIAS AND CROWN

Both the bias and the slope of the green cause the bowls to run in curved paths. The green will always tend to pull the bowl in the direction of the downward slope (see diagram opposite). As the bias can be transferred from one side of the bowl to the other, the two effects of bias and green can be used together to enhance the curving path, or against each other to make the bowl run almost straight. In the last foot (30cm) or so before the bowl stops, the pull of the bias at low speed will usually be much greater than the pull of the green, and the bowl will curve round in response to the bias.

The crowd watching the Wigan subs classic game.

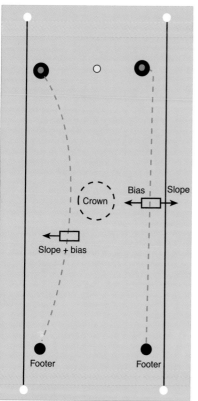

The round peg shot (left) sees the slope and bias used together to increase the bowl's curving path. The straight peg shot (right) sees the slope and bias work against each other to create an almost straight shot.

DELIVERY

Whichever hand a player uses to bowl the jack must then be used throughout the game to deliver subsequent jacks and bowls. The same side foot must also be on the footer when delivering a jack or a bowl. The only exception allowed is for a disabled player who suffers a permanent disability of a limb. If a player changes hands, the referee should order the bowl stopped and replayed properly the first time. If it occurs again, the bowl wrongly played shall be forfeited.

THE GAME

The game is played by two players, each normally playing two bowls alternately. The object is to get one or both bowls nearer to the jack than either of the opponent's bowls. Players score one point for each of their bowls nearer the jack than their opponent's. The number of points to be scored to win the game is agreed by the players before play starts.

The leader

The leader is the player who has the first attempt to set a mark and who delivers the first bowl. The winner of the coin toss becomes the leader for the first end. The winner of an end becomes the next end's leader. The leader places the footer within 3m of the green entrance and 1m from the green's edge. After the end finishes, the footer is placed within a 1m radius of the jack by the player becoming the leader of the next end.

Throughout the game each player must continue to use the jack and the bowls with which they started, except by permission of the referee, and then only if in the referee's opinion the jack or bowls are so damaged as to be unplayable.

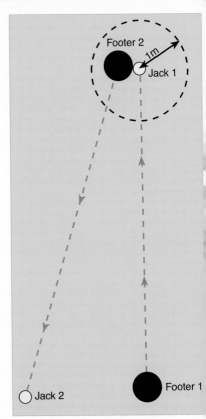

The footer for a new end (footer 2) must be placed within a 1m radius of the jack of the previous end.

SETTING A MARK

A legal delivery of the jack is called setting a mark. If leaders fail to set a mark, their opponent attempts to do so. If the opponent fails, attempts are made alternately until a mark is set, but the original leader always plays the first bowl. A mark is not set if:

- after an objection, the nearest point of the jack is measured to be less than 19m from the centre of the footer

- the jack goes off the green.

OBJECTION TO MARK

Verbal objection to a mark must be made after the first bowl has come to rest. If, after an objection to a mark has been made, it is proved by measurement to be a mark, the jack and bowl shall remain. If the leader fails to set a mark, objection to an attempt by the opponent must be made by the leader before delivering the first bowl.

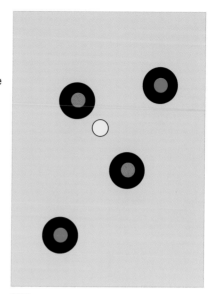

With both bowls nearer the jack than the opponent's, the red player scores two points.

> **The winner of an end is the only person allowed to signal the result to the markers.**

Gary Ellis 'setting a mark' with the jack.

JACK AND BOWL DELIVERY

The delivery of the jack is an important part of the game. As it runs over the green, it responds to the surface and to its own bias. The player can gain much information about the irregularities and the shape of the green by watching the jack. Leaders also get to choose which bias, finger or thumb, to give to the jack, but must not prevent their opponent from watching their delivery or the path of the jack from the footer.

JACK OFF GREEN

If the jack is struck off the green, the end is considered over and play resumes 1m from where the jack went off the green. The player who set the mark, delivers the jack again.

JACK IMPEDED OR DISPLACED

There are often several games taking place simultaneously on the green. As each game proceeds criss-cross over the green, interference may takes place. The jack must be returned and delivered again if:

- while it is still running it is impeded or
- it stops in the direct path of the bowls of another game.

If two jacks from different games are bowled near the same place, the last one to come to rest is not a mark and is returned to the players.

When a mark has been set, the end becomes void if:

- the jack is displaced by a bowl or the jack of another player or
- the jack is displaced by an outside cause and the players cannot agree on its position
- the jack is struck by a player's bowl and hits any person on the green
- the jack is struck by a player's bowl and hits a jack or bowl belonging to another game.

DELIVERING THE BOWL

Each player can retain possession of the footer until their bowl has ceased running. Many players complete their delivery by following up the bowl. If the opponent should then take possession of the footer, the opponent must wait until the bowl has stopped running before delivering their own bowl.

DEAD BOWL

A bowl that becomes dead must be taken out of play immediately. A bowl becomes dead if:

- it travels less than 3m from the footer

- it is played or struck off the green

- it falls out of the player's hand and runs so far that it cannot be recovered without leaving the footer

- it is placed, not played

- a bowl other than the player's own is delivered.

 Graeme Wilson, the 2003 Champion of Champions, in action.

RUNNING BOWL IMPEDED

If a running bowl is impeded by either player, both the offending player's bowls shall be forfeited at that end.

If a running bowl is impeded, other than by a player, it must be played again. If the bowl is the leader's first, the leader can choose to also set a new mark with the jack.

APPROACHING A RUNNING BOWL

If following the bowl across the green, the player must give their opponent a clear view of the bowl's path. If players are standing at the end where the jack lies, they must not stand directly behind the jack or obstruct their opponent's view.

The first time a player tries to speed up or slow down their bowl, it is taken out of play. If players reoffend, their bowls are removed from the green and the game is awarded to their opponent. They receive no further score.

Lee Lawton following his bowl down the rink.

PLAYING WRONG BOWL

A bowl played out of turn must be returned and replayed in its correct turn. If a bowl other than the player's own is delivered, by mistake or deliberately, it becomes a dead bowl and the following actions occur:

- the player loses one of their bowls as a penalty

- the bowl is returned to the opponent to be played again by its proper owner

- if the bowl disturbs the jack or another bowl in play, they should be replaced to their original position or as near as possible.

> **If you see a running jack or bowl from your game is likely to strike a bowl or jack from another game, try to stop the jack or bowl which should be returned and replayed.**

MEASURING TAPE OBSTRUCTION

If a mark has been set, but the leader cannot deliver the first bowl because a tape is on the green while a mark in another game is measured, the jack can be returned and another mark set.

A player being carefully watched as he throws out the jack.

DISTURBING A STILL BOWL

Should either player touch or displace a still bowl before the end is completed, both the offending players' bowls are forfeited at that end. If a still bowl is disturbed by any other person it must be replaced as near as possible to its original position. Similar action is taken if a still bowl is disturbed by a jack or bowl from another game.

COUNTING THE SCORE

Neither jack nor bowls can be moved until the players are agreed on the result, otherwise the opponent can claim a point for each of his bowls in play.

When bowls rest on one another, measuring without removing the obstructing bowl can be impossible. Such removals should always be made by the referee. If the remaining bowl moves its position when the supporting bowl is removed, the player must accept its new position.

REFEREE'S FUNCTIONS

The functions of the referee are to:

- settle any dispute not provided for in the laws of the game
- insist on adherence to the laws of the game
- give decisions when the players cannot agree
- remove a bowl so that measuring can be carried out.

Don't disturb the jack or bowls when measuring. If you do, you will lose the point you are trying to claim.

A crown green game in action at the Spring Waterloo 2008.

CONDUCT

Unfair play, impolite conduct or willful breaches of the laws should be punished severely by the referee, whose decision is final. On the first occasion, the referee may caution the player concerned or order them to retire from the green. On the second occasion, the referee should send the offender off the green. The punished player forfeits the game and receives no score, and their opponent is awarded the maximum score.

Good behaviour is expected of spectators. Only the players, referee and the measurers are allowed on the green.

INTERRUPTIONS

Once a game has started it should be played to its finish. Players may temporarily leave the green having informed their opponent and obtained the permission of the referee. If they fail to get permission, they forfeit the game. If bad light or the weather causes an interruption or postponement of the game, the points scored by each player will continue to count. The position of the jack on the green should be marked so that the game can be resumed from its interrupted point. Appeals for play to be stopped because of the light or the weather should be made to the referee.

ASSOCIATIONS

For further information on the game of bowls, contact:

Bowls England
Lyndhurst Road
Worthing
West Sussex
BN11 2AZ

www.bowlsengland.com

British Crown Green Bowling Association
94 Fishers Lane
Pensby
Wirral
CH61 8SB

www.bowls.org

The basic crown green scoreboard.

BOWLS CHRONOLOGY

1903 English Bowling Association (EBA) founded and the first Annual International match takes place in London.

1907 British Crown Green Bowling Association (BCGBA) was founded.

1908 BCGBA Senior County Championship began.

1910 BCGBA Senior Individual Merit began.

1911 British Parks Crown Green Bowling Association was founded.

1912 The EBA National Pairs competition introduced.

1923 New EBA regulations introduced for the official testing of bowls.

1933 Rules of the EBA (Indoor section) agreed and adopted.

1962 British Isles Bowling Council is formed.

1966 England plays in first World Bowls Competition where D. J. Bryant won the first gold medal.

1969 British Crown Green Ladies Bowling Association was founded.

1972 Second World Bowls Championships held in Worthing.

1974 BCGBA Junior Individual Merit began.

1974 BCGBA Champion of Champions began.

1976 National Umpires Association formed.

1984 BCGBA Junior County Championship began.

1991 BCGBA Veterans Championship began.

1991 First Junior International Trial Match held in Leicestershire.

1993 BCGBA Club Championship began.

1995 BCGBA Veterans County Championship began.

2007 BCGBA Centenary Mixed Pairs Championship began.

2008 Unification of the EBA and EWBA into Bowls England.

GLOSSARY

Backhand When, for the right-handed player, the bowl is delivered so that the curve of the bowl is from left to right towards the jack.

Bias The means by which the bowl travels in a curve.

Centre line An imaginary line that runs lengthwise down the centre of the rink.

Dead bowl A bowl that comes to rest in the ditch or is knocked into the ditch and is not a toucher or a bowl that comes outside the confines of the rink.

Delivery The action when the bowl leaves the hand.

Drawing the shot A bowl delivered at the correct pace or weight, and with the correct green or land, to arrive exactly at the objective.

End The sequence of play beginning with the placing of the mat and ending when the last player's bowl comes to rest.

Foot fault The player shall have all or part of one foot on or above the mat at the moment they deliver the bowl or jack.

Head The jack and any bowls that have come to rest within the boundaries of the rink of play and are not dead.

Jack (or kitty) The round white or yellow ball towards which the play is directed.

Lead The player who places the mat, rolls the jack and delivers the first bowl in any end.

Live bowl Any bowl that comes to rest within the confines of the rink or any toucher in the ditch.

Mark (or chalk) it The marking of a toucher with chalk or spray chalk.

Marker A person who, in a game of singles, ensures that the game is played in accordance with Laws, marks all touchers, centres the jack, measures when asked and keeps the score.

Mat line The edge of the mat nearest to the front ditch.

Pace (or weight) The amount of force with which the bowl is delivered to execute a particular shot.

Rink A rectangular area of green not more then 5.8m or less than 4.3m wide on which play takes place.

Second The second (or two) keeps the scorecard and scoreboard up to date.

Shot The bowl that finishes nearest to the jack at any stage of play.

Shoulder of the green The point on the green where the bowl begins to curve towards its objective.

Skip The player who captains the fours, triples or pairs. He is the last to bowl and is responsible for dictating the tactics of the game.

Stance The position adopted by the bowler on the mat prior to delivery.

Third The third (or three) advises the skip on choice of shots, and agrees the number of shots scored, measuring if required.

Tied end When the nearest bowls of each side are exactly the same distance from (or are touching) the jack. Neither side scores, but it is a completed end, and should be entered on the scorecard with no score being awarded to either side.

Toucher A bowl which during its course had touched the jack or a bowl which has come to rest and falls over to touch the jack before the next bowl is delivered. Touchers should be marked with a chalk mark before the next bowl delivered comes to rest.

Umpire The person with the authority during a game to enforce the Laws of the Sport of Bowls.

Wick (off) A bowl travelling at a certain pace which comes into an angled contact with another bowl so that the direction taken by the bowl is definitely altered.

INDEX